FOOLPROOF

• AIR FRYER •

FOOLPROOF

AIR FRYER

60 QUICK AND EASY RECIPES
THAT LET THE FRYER DO THE WORK

LOUISE KENNEY

PHOTOGRAPHY BY
RITA PLATTS

Hardie Grant

QUADRILLE

Managing Director
Sarah Lavelle

Commissioning Editor
Stacey Cleworth

Project Editor
Vicky Orchard

Series Designer
Emily Lapworth

Designer
Katy Everett

Photographer
Rita Platts

Food Stylist
Louise Kenney

Food Stylist Assistants
Sophie Denmead,
Jemima Mills, Luke
Felix-Wood, Ayala Daly

Prop Stylist
Max Robinson

Head of Production
Stephen Lang

**Senior Production
Controller**
Sabeena Atchia

First published in 2023 by Quadrille,
an imprint of Hardie Grant Publishing

Quadrille
52–54 Southwark Street
London SE1 1UN
quadrille.com

Text © Louise Kenney 2023
Photography © Rita Platts 2023
Design and layout © Quadrille 2023

Cataloguing in Publication Data: a catalogue
record for this book is available from the
British Library.

978 1 78713 967 1

Printed in China

MIX
Paper from
responsible sources
FSC™ C020056
FSC
www.fsc.org

CONTENTS

INTRODUCTION

Air fryers are here to stay. Once a newfangled kitchen gadget, they have quickly become mainstream and have worked their way into recipe methods from magazines to foodie websites. They are a brilliant and handy addition to any kitchen simply because they are so fast to heat up (typically they take 3 minutes to reach your desired temperature, versus 10–15 minutes for a conventional oven) and they cook food more quickly. For example, a 1.6kg (3lb 8oz) chicken roasts in 1 hour in an air fryer, whereas a conventional oven takes 1 hour 20 minutes. Speedy! If you are keen to get cracking already, try out the Whole Roast Chicken recipe on page 67.

At the time of writing, we are deep in a cost of living crisis, with all households making a concerted effort to cook more economically. Our family of six have found an air fryer to be really useful, not just for making our energy consumption more efficient, but also for helping to feed ourselves nutritious food in very little time. It preheats in minutes and makes weeknight cooking convenient and mostly hands-off. Air frying needs you to occasionally turn the food to ensure it cooks evenly – this is easy to do with tongs or simply by giving the basket a gentle shake part way through cooking.

I am a cook-from-scratch kind of person and I have to admit I was sceptical at first (we don't even own a microwave!) but the more I got to know my air fryer, the more I enjoyed experimenting with it. Now I always ask myself, 'Can I cook this in the air fryer?' With a few exceptions, the answer is usually 'yes'. From baked

potatoes and calamari to raspberry cupcakes and loaded nachos, this book has recipes for every appetite.

All of the recipes have been developed using both a single basket-style (5.2-litre/21-cup) air fryer and an oven-style one. Both have their advantages – the oven-style air fryer is great for baking and for getting food really crispy as there is a larger surface area, along with 3 cooking racks (mine also came with a rotisserie stick for roasting a whole chicken). My favourite to use, however, is the basket-style model with a removable crisper plate. It's really versatile – you can cook on the base of the basket, meaning you can make some saucy dishes – not just crispy ones. It is also very easy to clean.

Some air fryers have preset function buttons (bake, roast, air fry, dehydrate and so on) with built-in timers on them, however, I found it easiest to set the temperature I wanted and then adjust the timer. This gave me more accuracy with each recipe.

How an air fryer differs from an oven

Air fryers use convection (just like a conventional oven) to cook food; however, the fan is situated at the top of the appliance, rather than at the back. The heating element emits air into the cooking chamber while a fan circulates the hot air around it, creating a high-intensity convection oven. The air distribution makes food crisp up, achieving similar results to deep-fat frying – but don't be fooled, you still need to use some oil to ensure perfectly golden food, just not litres of the stuff!

What an air fryer does best

Quick and crispy was my mantra when writing the recipes for this book. But while wonderful at making things crispy – see recipes for Skin-On Chunky Chips on page 116, Courgette & Parmesan Fries on page 29 and even Roast Potatoes on page 100 – air fryers are also excellent (and reliable) for roasting joints of meat (see page 92 for Spiced Rack of Lamb and page 64 for Roast Pork). Chicken thighs are also an air fryer's best friend – just make sure they have the skin on for ultimate crispiness. I've also created lots of smaller snack recipes for when you have people over – try the Parmesan & Anchovy Twists on page 22 or the Spiced Roasted Almonds on page 16.

Air fryers are great for cooking for small children and 1–2 person households because you can cook a whole meal in one go, making the air fryer a bit of a one-pot appliance. If you have a double-drawer model, then you can cook two recipes simultaneously or make larger quantities. They are perfect for making one element of a meal while you prepare the rest, either on the hob or with no cooking at all. To this end, I've created a list of simple no-cook side dishes (see pages 118–119), which can help elevate a smaller recipe into a satisfying meal. You could also combine the side dishes with a number of the recipes from the Snacks and Light Bites chapters to create a mezze, for instance:

Warm Red Pepper & Walnut Dip (page 18)

Calamari (page 21)

Falafel (page 38)

Prawn, Red Pepper & Garlic Butter Skewers (page 57)

Garlic Yogurt with Sumac (page 118)

Couscous (page 119)

A note on ingredients

Where possible (and if funds allow) please consider buying organic or free-range ingredients, especially meat, eggs and dairy. I have a simple scale when buying food for our family: first choice: local business and organic produce; second choice: organic produce; third choice: local business. Obviously this isn't possible all of the time, but we all have a part to play in protecting our environment through our food choices and energy consumption.

Tips & tricks

Do consult the manufacturer's manual to give you some help, as air fryers take some getting used to. As with all appliances, models vary, so you will need to do some experimenting to see what works best for yours.

Shake, shake!

Many of the recipes in this book ask you to shake the basket halfway through cooking, as this encourages the air to circulate and all the food to cook evenly. You can also use tongs to turn the food, if you prefer.

Fat

Make sure you brush the food with some oil before cooking. You can use either a cooking oil spray or just a good old pastry brush and a jar of oil. In some instances you'll need to spray the basket or tray before transferring food but each recipe will tell you what to do. For crispy dishes requiring a high temperature, use a sunflower oil or vegetable oil spray. Olive oil is best used at lower temperatures.

Essential items

Here is a list of things I like to use, which are useful to have around when you're using an air fryer; you'll likely have many of these already and they will make life much easier when cooking the recipes in this book:

- wooden or silicone-tipped tongs
- traditional or silicone pastry brush
- cooking oil spray (sunflower or vegetable oil)
- pre-cut perforated air-fryer parchment liners or a perforated silicone liner
- parchment cake tin liners
- silicone 6-hole cupcake tray
- cake tin which fits inside your air fryer
- roasting tin which fits inside your air fryer
- heatproof trivet or mat
- meat probe or thermometer (for checking meat such as chicken is fully cooked – an internal temperature of 74°C (165°F) is considered fully cooked for poultry).

Do's & don'ts

DO preheat your air fryer (this takes about 3 minutes).

DON'T preheat your air fryer with baking parchment inside, otherwise the paper will get sucked up to the heating element and could cause a kitchen fire!

DON'T overload your air fryer, otherwise the food won't crisp up.

DO use tongs to lift food out of the air fryer.

DO use an oven mitt if you have to reach in to remove a baking tin.

DO read the manual of your air fryer as all models differ.

DO make use of the timer on your air fryer to remind you when you shake the basket/turn food/check if the food is cooked.

DO clean your air fryer between uses as the fats can build up.

A NOTE ON SYMBOLS

Each recipes tells you if it is vegetarian, vegan or can be made vegan. I have also given guidance on which recipes suit which type of air fryer and, in most cases, I've given you instructions for what to do if you don't have the air fryer type best suited to the recipe.

V = vegetarian

VE = vegan

VO = vegan option given

 best suited to a basket-style air fryer

 best suited to an oven-style air fryer

All recipes serve between 1–4 people.

SNACKS

This chapter is great if you are entertaining and want some simple snacks to go round with a drink. Many of these recipes are made to be shared and some of them take less than 15 minutes to prepare and cook.

DRIED APPLE RINGS OR MANGO SLICES VE

Dried fruit made at home is so much more satisfying to eat than the shop-bought version. Do experiment with other ingredients like strawberries, pears and apricot halves; you'll need to adjust the timing but see what happens. There's no need to peel or core the apples here unless you prefer skinless apple rings. These are great as a healthy snack on their own but also delicious dipped in plain yogurt or spread with peanut butter. If you like shop-bought dried mango, then this recipe will work well for you. You can vary the cooking time – increasing the time will give you a crispy mango 'chip', whereas reducing the cooking time gives you squishier, soft dried mango. You will need 2–3 racks for this recipe.

3 sharp eating apples (Granny Smith or Braeburn), sliced into 3–4mm (⅛–¼ in) rings
or 1–2 ripe mangoes, peeled and cut into 5mm (¼in) thick slices

Lay out the apple or mango slices on 2–3 racks; the slices can touch but not overlap as you want them to dry evenly.

Dehydrate the apple rings at 50°C (125°F) for 4 hours or the mango slices for 3 hours.

The apple rings will keep in an airtight container for up to 2 weeks and the mango slices will keep for up to a week.

Serves 2–4
–
Prep 5 mins
–
Cook 3–4 hrs

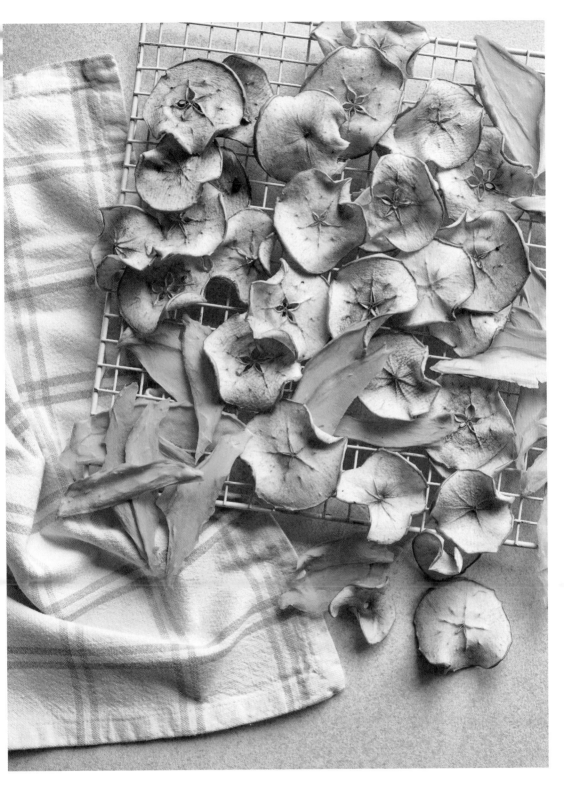

FRUIT LEATHER VE

A great alternative to shop-bought fruit roll-ups for children and more economical than using your oven. You can make this using one type of berry or a mixture, as in the recipe below. Defrosted frozen berries work well here too. If you have two racks in your air fryer you could make two batches at once, but you will need to swap the racks around halfway through cooking, as the bottom rack often cooks more slowly.

250g (9oz) mixed berries, such as strawberries, blueberries and raspberries

Blend the berries in a food processor, or using a stick blender, until puréed. Sieve out any seeds, leaving you with a smooth purée (skip this step if you, or your kids, don't mind the seeds).

Line the air fryer with some non-stick baking parchment or an air-fryer liner.

Spread the berry purée onto the parchment in an even layer, not quite to the edges, and dehydrate at 60°C (140°F) for 5 hours. Check it after 4 hours, as some air fryers are more efficient. It is ready when it is no longer sticky when pressed. If it is still sticky, then return to the air fryer for another hour.

Leave to cool, then peel off the fruit leather and cut into 2cm (¾in) thick strips. These will keep in an airtight container for up to 2 weeks.

Serves 4
–
Prep 5 mins
–
Cook 5 hrs

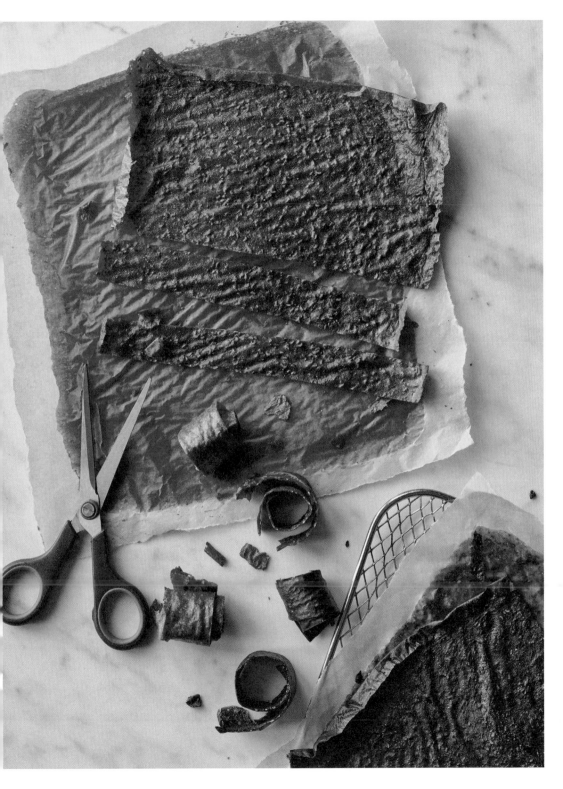

SPICED ROASTED ALMONDS VE

A fantastic snack which takes seconds to prepare and is ready in a matter of minutes. A lovely alternative to shop-bought nuts and much healthier! You could substitute cashews for almonds if you prefer.

300g (10½oz) whole almonds
1 tbsp olive oil
½ tsp chipotle chilli flakes
½ tsp sweet smoked paprika
½ tsp ground cumin
½ tsp ground coriander
1 tsp mixed dried herbs
1½ tsp sea salt
freshly ground black pepper

Preheat your air fryer to 190°C (375°F).

Mix the almonds with the remaining ingredients and ensure all the nuts are coated in the spices and oil.

Pour the almonds into a tin which fits your air fryer and spread out in an even layer. Set the timer to 5 minutes. If using a basket, shake it halfway through cooking to ensure the nuts toast evenly.

Remove and set aside to cool.

These will keep in an airtight container for up to 2 weeks, although I'd be surprised if they last that long!

Serves 4
–
Prep 2 mins
–
Cook 5 mins

WARM RED PEPPER & WALNUT DIP VE

This sweet, creamy dip is best served warm with a little extra virgin olive oil slaked over the top and some extra chopped walnuts for decoration. You can use an air-fryer liner if you like, but it's not essential. This is best eaten as soon as it's made, and crusty bread or crudités are the perfect, easy vehicle for this dip.

3 garlic cloves, peeled
1 large red (bell) pepper, cut in half and deseeded
70g (2½oz) walnuts, plus extra chopped, to serve
80ml (2½fl oz/⅓ cup) extra virgin olive oil
1 tbsp pomegranate molasses
sea salt and freshly ground black

Preheat the air fryer to 190°C (375°F).

Put the garlic into the air fryer and place the pepper halves on top, enclosing the garlic so it doesn't burn. Bake for 7 minutes, then tip in the walnuts and bake for another 6 minutes until the skin of the peppers has blistered.

Transfer the peppers to a bowl and cover with foil or cling film (plastic wrap). Leave to steam for 5 minutes, then pull away and discard the skins.

Transfer the peppers, garlic, walnuts, oil and pomegranate molasses to a food processor. Sprinkle over some salt and pepper, then blitz until creamy and a little like hummus.

Transfer to a bowl, scatter over some chopped walnuts and enjoy with some good bread or crudités. Store any leftovers in an airtight container in the fridge for 2–3 days.

Serves 4
–
Prep 10 mins
–
Cook 13 mins

CALAMARI

Enjoying this crispy calamari reminds me of being on holiday; it's so quick and easy to make but it feels decadent to eat. You could happily double the quantities to serve 4; all you need to do is cook them in two batches and eat the first batch while the second is cooking! These would be fantastic served with a chilled glass of Albariño or a sparkling wine. Great served with either of the mayonnaise recipes on page 118. This recipe is best made in a basket air fryer.

300g (10½oz) squid rings (if using frozen, defrost first)
3 tbsp olive oil
30g (1oz) panko breadcrumbs
zest of 1 lemon (reserve the rest of the lemon to serve)
sea salt and freshly ground black pepper

Drain the squid of any excess liquid, then, in a large bowl, mix the squid rings with the olive oil.

In a separate, shallow bowl, or deep baking tray, mix the panko breadcrumbs with the lemon zest, a good pinch of salt and some black pepper.

Dust each squid ring with the breadcrumb mixture, ensuring each ring is coated evenly.

Preheat the air fryer to 190°C (375°F).

Tip the squid rings into the air fryer and cook for 7 minutes, giving them a gentle shake halfway through.

Serve immediately with some mayonnaise and a good squeeze of lemon juice.

Serves 2
–
Prep 5 mins
–
Cook 7 mins

LOADED NACHOS VO

This is such an easy vegetarian dish and really satisfying to tuck into. The tomatoes cook down a little and layering it up means all the tortilla chips get a good slathering of toppings. You could substitute the Gouda for grated vegan mozzarella and vegan sour cream if you like. You will need a deep baking dish which fits your air fryer for this recipe, along with a parchment cake tin liner.

250g (9oz) cherry tomatoes, quartered
½ red onion, finely chopped
1 red chilli, finely chopped (keep the seeds in if you like the heat!)
1 tsp red wine vinegar
1 tbsp olive oil
1 small bunch of coriander (cilantro), finely chopped
200g (7oz) salted tortilla chips
200g (7oz) Gouda slices
2 tbsp jalapeños from a jar, drained
3 spring onions (scallions), finely sliced
sea salt and freshly ground black pepper
sour cream, to serve

In a small bowl, mix together the cherry tomatoes, red onion, red chilli, red wine vinegar, olive oil and half the coriander (cilantro).

Preheat the air fryer to 180°C (350°F) and line a deep baking tin with a parchment cake tin liner (this will make removing the nachos easier).

Tip half the tortilla chips into the lined tin, then top with half the tomato mixture, half the cheese and half the jalapeños. Repeat to make a second layer.

Air-fry for 8 minutes.

Carefully remove the nachos from the baking dish, taking hold of the exposed bits of parchment, and transfer to a serving dish. Sprinkle over the remaining coriander and the sliced spring onions (scallions) and serve immediately with a good dollop of sour cream.

Serves 4
–
Prep 5 mins
–
Cook 8 mins

ROOT VEG CRISPS VE

A fantastic way to use up your root veg peelings instead of throwing them away – just make sure the vegetables have been well scrubbed before you peel them – you don't want to chow down on soil! Parsnips, carrots, potatoes and beetroot all work fantastically here. If you have more than 150g (5½oz) peelings, cook them in batches, as overcrowding the air fryer will prevent the pieces from crisping up.

150g (5½oz) root veg peelings (from about 1kg/2lb 4oz washed root veg)
1 tbsp olive oil
½ tsp sea salt

Preheat the air fryer to 200°C (400°F).

Soak the vegetable peelings in cold water for 5 minutes.

Drain well, then pat dry on kitchen paper. This part is key to getting crispy crisps!

In a large bowl, mix the peelings with the olive oil and salt, ensuring they are well coated.

Air-fry for 6 minutes, giving the basket a good shake halfway through to ensure they all crisp up evenly.

NOTE: If you are using an oven-style air fryer, spread the peelings out in a single layer and check them halfway through – you may only need to cook them for 5 minutes.

Serves 2
–
Prep 7 mins
–
Cook 6 mins

PARMESAN & ANCHOVY TWISTS

I have made these so many times and they always go down well. These could, like the filo rolls on page 44, pass as canapés. Don't worry about keeping the twists straight – curly, and wonky straws are just as delicious! Just ensure they are spaced apart so they can puff up and get crispy. This recipe is best made using two racks in an oven-style air fryer, but you can still make them in a basket air fryer – just bake them in batches.

1 × 320g (11¼oz) sheet of ready-rolled all-butter puff pastry
1 tsp Dijon mustard mixed with 1 tsp water
1 × 50g (1¾oz) can anchovies
20g (¾oz) Parmesan, freshly grated

Lay the pastry sheet out and cut it in half. Using a pastry brush, paint the Dijon mixture over the surface of one of the sheets.

Shake off any excess oil from the anchovies and lay them in 3 rows, about 2cm (¾in) apart, on top of the Dijon.

Sprinkle over the Parmesan, then lay the plain pastry sheet on top. Press down with your hands to seal, and roll out gently, just to make sure everything has stuck together.

Refrigerate for 15 minutes.

Preheat the air fryer to 200°C (400°F).

Cut the pastry into 1cm (½in) wide strips, at 90 degrees to the anchovy rows, so you get little bits of anchovy in each strip.

Twist each strip in opposite directions a few times and press down the ends onto the work surface to help them keep their shape. Bake, spaced apart, for 12 minutes, swapping the racks halfway through.

Serves 4
–
Prep 5 mins,
15 mins chilling
–
Cook 12 mins

COURGETTE & PARMESAN FRIES

A lighter and more elegant version of potato fries, these go beautifully with either of the mayonnaise recipes on page 118. This is another nice recipe to serve as a snack with drinks – just make sure you serve them as soon as they are made as they can go soggy if left for more than 15 minutes.

1 large courgette (zucchini), about
    250g (9oz)
2 tbsp freshly grated Parmesan
60g (2¼oz) panko breadcrumbs
½ tsp dried rosemary
½ tsp dried thyme
40g (1½oz) plain (all-purpose) flour
1 small egg, beaten with 1 tbsp cold
    water
sea salt and freshly ground black
    pepper

Preheat the air fryer to 190°C (375°F).

Cut the courgette (zucchini) into batons about 10 × 1cm (4 x ½in).

Mix together the Parmesan, breadcrumbs, dried rosemary and thyme.

Place the flour into a shallow bowl and season with salt and pepper. Put the beaten egg into a second shallow bowl and the breadcrumb mixture into a third.

Dip the courgette batons into the flour, then the egg, followed by the breadcrumbs.

Place into the air fryer and bake for 10 minutes. If using a basket air fryer, shake the basket halfway through.

Serves 2
–
Prep 10 mins
–
Cook 10 mins

WARM AUBERGINE DIP VO

This is such a simple snack and is delicious served with some dukkah (page 118) sprinkled over the top. Great for entertaining or slathered on toast for lunch. It would also work nicely with the Garlic & Nigella Seed Bread on page 105.

1 medium aubergine (eggplant), pricked all over with a knife
60g (2¼oz) Greek or vegan yogurt
juice of 1 lemon
1 garlic clove, crushed
1 tbsp extra virgin olive oil
2 tbsp tahini
sea salt and freshly ground black pepper
Dukkah (page 118), to serve

Preheat the air fryer to 190°C (375°F).

Air-fry the whole aubergine (eggplant) for 25 minutes.

Remove and set aside for a couple of minutes until it is cool enough to handle. Peel away (and discard) the skin and trim off the top. Roughly chop the flesh, then place into a bowl along with the remaining ingredients.

Mix briefly, then blitz with a stick blender until smooth.

Serve on toast sprinkled with dukkah.

<table>
<tr><td>Serves 4</td></tr>
<tr><td>–</td></tr>
<tr><td>Prep 5 mins</td></tr>
<tr><td>–</td></tr>
<tr><td>Cook 25 mins</td></tr>
</table>

CAJUN SWEET POTATO FRIES VE

Fries are a staple air fryer recipe and these are no exception. Great served with the garlic yogurt on page 118 or alongside the aubergine dip on page 30. You could also double the recipe and serve them as a side with the Whole Roast Chicken on page 67.

2 × 300g (10½oz) sweet potatoes, peeled and cut into 5mm (¼in) thick fries
2 tbsp olive oil
1 tsp sea salt
1 tsp smoked sweet paprika
1 tsp garlic powder
½ tsp dried oregano or thyme
½ tsp freshly ground black pepper
¼ tsp chilli flakes

Preheat the air fryer to 200°C (400°F).

Using your hands, mix together the sweet potato fries with the olive oil, salt and all the spices. Make sure all the fries are well coated in the oil and spices.

Transfer half the fries to the air fryer and air-fry for 15 minutes, shaking the basket halfway through. Repeat with the remaining fries.

Serve immediately.

Serves 2
–
Prep 5 mins
–
Cook 30 mins

LIGHT BITES

Here I've created recipes which work well for lunch as well as giving you options for more substantial snacks. Have a look at The Ultimate Cheese Toastie or the Prawn, Red Pepper & Garlic Butter Skewers. Dishes like the Spicy Chicken Wings are a great Friday night feasting snack. For vegan options check out the Falafel, Onion Bhajis and Bang Bang Cauliflower.

BAKED CAMEMBERT WITH TOASTS v

This is best made using a Camembert in a wooden container. If you can't find one, just create a foil container for the Camembert using two layers of foil, leaving the top exposed. This could pass as a sharing-style canapé to serve 4–6 people.

150g (5½oz) par-baked baguette, sliced into 1cm (½in) slices
1 tbsp olive oil
250g (9oz) Camembert
1 garlic clove, thickly sliced
3 rosemary sprigs, cut into 2cm (¾in) lengths
sea salt

Preheat the air fryer to 180°C (350°F).

In a large bowl, mix the baguette slices with the olive oil and a good pinch of sea salt.

Air-fry for 6 minutes, shaking the basket halfway through so all the pieces brown evenly. Set aside while you make the Camembert.

Unwrap the cheese and cut several deep slits into the top. Stud the cheese with the garlic slices and the rosemary.

Air-fry for 10 minutes.

Let the cheese sit for a couple of minutes before serving with the toasts.

Serves 2
–
Prep 5 mins
–
Cook 16 mins

FALAFEL VE

Falafel are so nutritious and tasty – I much prefer home-made ones to shop-bought. Ideal as a snack or light lunch stuffed into a warm pitta with extra tahini, lemon juice and some baby salad leaves. You could transform this into a meal for two by serving with the couscous, tomato salsa and vegan mayonnaise on pages 118–119.

1 × 400g (14oz) can chickpeas (garbanzos), drained
1 tbsp tahini
1 tbsp extra virgin olive oil
1 small onion, roughly chopped
2 garlic cloves, peeled
small mixed handful of fresh coriander (cilantro) and flat-leaf parsley, roughly chopped
½ tsp ground cumin
1 tsp ground coriander
pinch of salt
cooking oil spray
freshly ground black pepper

Preheat the air fryer to 200°C (400°F).

Place all of the ingredients, except the cooking oil, into a food processor and blend until finely chopped and combined.

Using wet hands, shape the mixture into 12 balls and flatten slightly with your fingers.

Spray the air fryer with a little cooking oil, then place the falafel into the air fryer and cook for 8 minutes.

Serve with some plain yogurt and pickles.

Serves 4
–
Prep 5 mins
–
Cook 8 mins

HALLOUMI & CHERRY TOMATO SKEWERS v

Halloumi eaten still warm from cooking is my idea of heaven – soft but chewy with a little crispiness. The honey adds some balance to the salty cheese. You could add more herbs to serve if you like – flat-leaf parsley would work well. You'll need six wooden skewers for this recipe.

225g (8oz) halloumi, cut into 24 pieces
12 cherry tomatoes, halved
olive oil, for brushing

To serve
runny honey
a few mint leaves
sesame or poppy seeds

Preheat the air fryer to 200°C (400°F). Trim 6 wooden skewers so that they fit your air fryer.

Thread the halloumi pieces and cherry tomatoes onto each skewer in any order you like. Brush the cheese and halloumi with a little olive oil.

Lay 3 skewers on the air fryer shelf and lay the remaining skewers on top at right angles so there is plenty of room for the air to circulate.

Bake for 5 minutes.

Remove the skewers with tongs and serve with runny honey drizzled over the top and a few torn mint leaves and some sesame or poppy seeds sprinkled over.

Serves 2
–
Prep 5 mins
–
Cook 5 mins

CAJUN-STYLE CHICKEN FILLETS

A bit like a Cajun version of takeaway chicken, these are filling and could easily be augmented to make a main meal if you add the coleslaw and garlic yogurt recipes from pages 118–119. Make sure you cut the chicken into similar-sized pieces so they all cook evenly.

650g (1lb 7oz) skinless chicken breasts, cut into 12–14 strips
sunflower or vegetable oil cooking spray

For the marinade
150g (5½oz) plain yogurt
zest and juice of 1 lemon
1 tsp smoked paprika
1 tsp black pepper
½ tsp sea salt
1 tsp garlic powder
½ tsp English mustard powder
½ tsp dried thyme
1 tbsp olive oil

For the panko crumb
2 tsp garlic powder
1 tbsp freshly ground black pepper
2 tsp smoked paprika
1 tsp sea salt
80g (2¾oz) panko breadcrumbs
½ tsp English mustard powder
1 tsp dried thyme

Mix the chicken strips with all the marinade ingredients, ensuring the chicken is well covered. Leave to marinate in the fridge for a couple of hours if possible.

Mix together the panko crumb ingredients, then spread out into a deep baking tray.

Working with a few chicken strips at a time, dip each piece into the panko mixture, turning them over so they are all evenly coated.

Preheat the air fryer to 200°C (400°F) and spray the basket with a little oil.

Place half the chicken pieces into the basket, leaving space in between each one, so they crisp up. Spray with a little more oil and cook for 14 minutes, turning them with tongs halfway through. Keep them warm under a clean tea towel while you cook the next batch.

Repeat with the remaining chicken pieces, then serve straight away.

Serves 4
–
Prep 15 mins
–
Cook 28 mins

FETA & PINE NUT FILO ROLLS

These rolls could easily pass for canapés, so serve them up alongside an apéritif to satisfy your hungry guests before lunch or dinner. Leave them to stand for a few minutes before serving, as the filling is hotter than the sun!

30g (1oz) Parmesan, grated
200g (7oz) feta, crumbled
zest and juice of 1 lemon
100g (3½oz) pine nuts
3 large mint sprigs, leaves only, roughly chopped
9 sheets of filo (phyllo) pastry, cut into 25cm (10in) squares
60g (2¼oz) melted butter
freshly ground black pepper

Place the Parmesan, feta, lemon zest and juice, pine nuts, chopped mint and plenty of black pepper into a food processor and blitz until well blended. It doesn't need to be totally smooth.

Starting with 3 sheets of filo pastry (keep the rest covered under a damp tea towel so they don't dry out), brush both sides of each sheet with the melted butter, then stack them on top of each other. Spoon the filling along the long edge to make a sausage, about 1cm (½in) thick. Tightly roll the pastry around the filling 1½ times, then cut along the long edge and brush with more butter to seal. Make another sausage with the remaining pastry stack and some more filling: you will get 2 long sausages out of each stack of 3 pastry sheets. Cut each long roll into 3 shorter sausages.

Repeat this process with the remaining pastry sheets and filling – you should end up with 18 rolls

Preheat the air fryer to 190°C (375°F) and bake the rolls, seam-side down, in two batches for 8 minutes. Keep warm under a clean tea towel while you bake the second batch.

Leave to cool for 5 minutes before tucking in.

Serves 6
–
Prep 25 mins
–
Cook 16 mins

Light Bites

CHORIZO & FENNEL SAUSAGE ROLLS

Chorizo and fennel are a match made in heaven. These are large sausage rolls so could easily be served as a main with salad and mustard on the side. Shop-bought sausages tend to have salt in them already, so there's no need to add any to the mixture.

1 × 320g (11¼oz) sheet ready-rolled all-butter puff pastry
5 pork sausages
60g (2¼oz) cooking chorizo, skin removed and finely chopped
5 thyme sprigs, leaves only
1 tsp fennel seeds
1 small egg, beaten
freshly ground black pepper

Unroll the puff pastry and cut it in half, giving you 2 squares.

In a bowl, squeeze the sausage meat out of the skins and mix together with the chorizo, thyme leaves, ½ teaspoon of the fennel seeds and lots of black pepper.

Split the mixture in half and roll into 2 sausage shapes, each about 14cm (5½in) long. Place each sausage in the middle of the pastry and trim away any excess pastry from the sides (you can use this for decoration if you like, so don't throw it away). Roll the pastry over the filling and press down the long edge to seal, cutting away any excess pastry. Crimp the sealed edge with a fork.

Preheat the air fryer to 200°C (400°F).

Brush the pastry liberally with the beaten egg and add any pastry decorations on top, then brush again with the egg.

Sprinkle over the remaining ½ teaspoon of fennel seeds and bake for 25 minutes until a deep golden brown and the filling is piping hot.

Leave for a couple of minutes, then serve.

Serves 2
–
Prep 10 mins
–
Cook 25 mins

SPICY CHICKEN WINGS

Sticky, messy and a pleasure to eat – you'll need napkins! If you can, try to marinate them for a few hours before air-frying, as the chicken soaks up the marinade flavours so well.

1kg (2lb 4oz) chicken wings
2 garlic cloves, crushed
2 tbsp chipotle paste
1 tbsp tomato purée (paste)
1 tbsp sriracha
1 tsp sea salt
2 tsp smoked paprika (use hot if you want your wings extra spicy)
3 tbsp red wine vinegar
2 tbsp soft brown sugar (light or dark)
2 tbsp olive oil
pinch of freshly ground black pepper

Trim the tip off each wing and discard (or collect them and make a small batch of chicken stock), then cut each wing in half, leaving you with wings and drumsticks.

Mix the remaining ingredients together in a large bowl, then tip the wings in and give everything a good mix, ensuring each wing is evenly coated.

If you have time, leave them to marinate in the fridge for a couple of hours, or overnight. This isn't essential, so crack on with air-frying them if you are short on time.

Preheat the air fryer to 200°C (400°F).

Tip half the wings into the air fryer, reserving any excess marinade, and cook for 12 minutes, shaking the basket halfway through cooking. Keep them warm under a clean tea towel while you cook the second batch.

Heat the reserved marinade in a saucepan until boiling. Simmer for 2–3 minutes, then mix with the cooked chicken wings and serve immediately.

ONION BHAJIS VO

This is a classic dish which is usually made by frying in hot oil – not so here! The air fryer works its magic, and these will become a staple in your kitchen. Quick to prepare and cook and very satisfying to eat – I am sure you will make these time and again.

100g (3½oz) gram (chickpea) flour
½ tsp ground turmeric
1 tsp ground cumin
2 tsp ground coriander
½ tsp cayenne pepper
1 garlic clove, crushed
1 small piece of fresh root ginger,
    peeled and finely grated
small bunch of fresh coriander
    (cilantro), finely chopped
2 red onions, finely sliced
1 tbsp rapeseed oil
100ml (3½fl oz/scant ½ cup) cold water
sea salt and freshly ground black
    pepper

To serve
4 tbsp plain yogurt, or vegan
    alternative
2 tbsp best-quality mango chutney
sliced red chilli
coriander (cilantro) leaves
lemon wedges

Preheat the air fryer to 190°C (375°F).

Mix together the flour, spices, crushed garlic, grated ginger and chopped coriander (cilantro).

Mix in the red onions, rapeseed oil and cold water along with a pinch of salt and some black pepper. Mix well to combine into a thick batter.

Spoon dessertspoonfuls of mixture into the hot air fryer, spaced apart, and fry for 8 minutes until crispy and golden. Keep warm under a clean tea towel while you cook the second batch.

Mix together the yogurt and mango chutney and serve alongside the hot bhajis, with some sliced red chilli, coriander leaves and lemon wedges alongside.

Serves 4
–
Prep 10 mins
–
Cook 16 mins

Light Bites

FISH FINGERS IN AN ALMOND CRUMB

A tasty gluten-free alternative to regular fish fingers. You can use any firm white fish, or even salmon if you prefer. You can serve them as suggested here or try either of the mayonnaise recipes on page 118. You could even dig out some tartare sauce from your fridge for a classic combination.

350g (12oz) skinless firm white fish fillets
2 tbsp plain (all-purpose) flour
1 egg, beaten with 1 tbsp cold water
70g (2½oz) ground almonds
finely grated zest of 1 lemon
cooking oil spray
sea salt and freshly ground black pepper

To serve
2 small flatbreads
Garlic Yogurt with Sumac (page 118)
4 cornichons, finely sliced
2 radishes, finely sliced
small handful of baby salad leaves
a few lemon wedges

Cut the fish into fingers about 1.5 × 10 cm (⅝ × 4in).

Place the flour into a shallow bowl and mix in a good pinch of salt and black pepper. In a second bowl, place the beaten egg and mix the ground almonds with the lemon zest in a third bowl.

Preheat the air fryer to 190°C (375°F).

Dip the fish fingers into the flour, then the egg and finally roll in the ground almonds.

Spray liberally with cooking oil, then transfer to the air fryer and cook for 7 minutes until golden.

Serve split between two flatbreads with the garlic yogurt, cornichons, radishes and salad leaves. Squeeze over some lemon juice and tuck in!

Serves 2
–
Prep 10 mins
–
Cook 7 mins

PESTO, OLIVE & PUFF PASTRY PARCELS

These super easy, store-cupboard pastries would be great as part of a mezze platter. They taste like summer even in the depths of winter. You could switch up the pesto – I have used a delicious aubergine (eggplant) pesto (thanks to my brother, Alex, for the tip-off) but you could use any type really – even a tapenade would work.

320g (11¼oz) sheet ready-rolled all-butter puff pastry
8 tsp aubergine (eggplant) pesto, or pesto of choice
12 pitted Kalamata olives, halved
4 sun-dried tomatoes, roughly chopped
16 marinated anchovies

To serve
Parmesan
Basil leaves

Unroll the pastry and cut it into 8 rectangles.

Spread 1 teaspoon of aubergine (eggplant) pesto over each rectangle, leaving a 1cm (½in) border. Top with 3 olive halves, a few pieces of sun-dried tomato and 2 anchovies.

Bring together two corners from opposite sides and pinch together to make an open pastry. Repeat this process with all the rectangles.

Preheat the air fryer to 190°C (375°F).

Line the air fryer with a perforated parchment liner and bake 4 pastries at a time, spaced apart (or as many as you can comfortably fit into your air fryer), for 9 minutes. Keep warm under a clean tea towel while you cook the second batch.

Serve immediately with a few Parmesan shavings and a couple of basil leaves.

Serves 4
–
Prep 5 mins
–
Cook 18 mins

PRAWN, RED PEPPER & GARLIC BUTTER SKEWERS

Incredibly easy and utterly delicious, you will want to make this recipe again and again. You could substitute olive oil for the butter and skip the melting stage if you want to save on washing up. You'll need six wooden skewers to make this dish. This recipe can be made in a basket or oven-style air fryer.

1 large red (bell) pepper, deseeded and cut into 24 pieces
200g (7oz) raw jumbo prawns (shrimp) (24 in total)
1 large red onion, cut into 24 pieces
75g (2½oz) chorizo ring, cut into 24 slices
50g (1¾oz) unsalted butter
2 garlic cloves, crushed
small bunch of flat-leaf parsley, finely chopped
sea salt and freshly ground black pepper

Preheat the air fryer to 190°C (375°F).

Cut 6 wooden skewers to fit inside your air fryer.

Thread each skewer with alternating pieces of pepper, prawn (shrimp), onion and chorizo.

Melt the butter over a gentle heat along with the garlic. Brush each skewer generously with the garlic butter and season well with salt and pepper.

Lay 3 skewers on the bottom of the air fryer and lay the remaining ones on top at right angles to the bottom layer.

Cook for 8 minutes, then remove and serve immediately, sprinkled with parsley.

Serves 2
–
Prep 10 mins
–
Cook 8 mins

Light Bites

THE ULTIMATE CHEESE TOASTIE

The coleslaw recipe on page 119 is the perfect zesty foil for this hot buttery sandwich. You could happily add a slice of good ham or some salami. Best served with some English mustard and some finely sliced red onion marinated for 5 minutes in cider or white wine vinegar.

butter, softened
2 slices of white sourdough, or bread of your choice
½ tsp Dijon mustard
1 tbsp red onion chutney
50g (1¾oz) Gruyère, grated
20g (¾oz) grated mozzarella
English mustard, to serve (optional)

Preheat the air fryer to 200°C (400°F).

Butter both sides of each slice of bread.

Arrange the slices side by side, then spread one slice with the Dijon and the other with the red onion chutney.

Sprinkle the Gruyère and mozzarella onto the Dijon slice, then top with the other, pressing down firmly.

Line the air fryer with a perforated parchment liner and lay the sandwich on top. Air-fry for 5 minutes until crisp on the outside and melted in the middle.

Serve immediately with some pickled onion (see intro) and English mustard, if you like.

Serves 1
–
Prep 3 mins
–
Cook 5 mins

BANG BANG CAULIFLOWER VO

Here the humble cauliflower is made into a surprisingly special dish. This, along with the Loaded Nachos on page 22, is perfect for sharing. Crunchy, salty, sweet and spiked with chilli, you will devour it in minutes.

1 × 400–500g (14oz–1lb 2oz) cauliflower, leaves removed and florets separated
130g (4½oz) plain (all-purpose) flour
1 tsp garlic powder
1 tsp sweet smoked paprika
½ tsp sea salt
pinch of freshly ground black pepper
1 tbsp toasted sesame oil
220ml (7½fl oz/scant 1 cup) milk of your choice
100g (3½oz) panko breadcrumbs
sunflower or vegetable cooking oil spray
juice of 1 lime, plus lime wedges to serve
1 tbsp sriracha
4 tbsp sweet chilli sauce
2 red chillies, finely chopped
2 spring onions (scallions), finely sliced
small bunch of fresh coriander (cilantro), finely chopped
1 tbsp sesame seeds

Cut the cauliflower florets into even-sized pieces – about 2cm (¾in) each.

In a bowl, mix together the flour, garlic powder, smoked paprika, salt and pepper, then whisk in the toasted sesame oil and milk until you have a smooth, thick batter.

Put the panko breadcrumbs into a deep baking tray (this will make coating the cauliflower easier).

Dunk the cauliflower florets into the batter, then roll each one in the panko breadcrumbs until all the pieces are coated.

Preheat the air fryer to 200°C (400°F).

Spray the basket with a little cooking oil, then place half the cauliflower florets (or as many as you can comfortably fit in) in a single layer, into the basket. Air-fry for 15 minutes, gently shaking halfway through to encourage all the sides to crisp up. Keep warm under a clean tea towel while you cook the second batch.

Meanwhile, mix together the lime juice, sriracha, sweet chilli sauce, red chillies, spring onions (scallions), coriander (cilantro) and sesame seeds to make a textured sauce.

Once all the cauliflower is cooked, arrange on a platter and spoon over the sauce. Serve immediately, with lime wedges for squeezing over.

Serves 4
–
Prep 20 mins
–
Cook 30 mins

MAINS

Air fryers are great for cooking meat and fish
– you'll find plenty of ideas here for speedy
weeknight meals, alongside more leisurely
options. Kids love the Squash Pasta Sauce
and the Chicken Schnitzel, and the Mushroom
Pithivier is fabulous if you are looking to impress.

ROAST PORK WITH APPLES & STAR ANISE

In this recipe, the pork roasts on top of a bed of vegetables and white wine, which gives you a lovely fruity sauce to serve alongside the roast meat. You can make this either directly on the bottom of your air fryer, or in an ovenproof dish which fits inside your air fryer – you want a container to collect the juices so that you end up with a self-made gravy.

1.3kg (3lb) pork loin crackling joint
1 large or 2 small cooking apples, peeled, cored and cut into 1cm (½in) slices
2 eating apples, peeled, cored and cut into 1cm (½in) slices
2 onions, peeled and cut into wedges
3 carrots, peeled and chopped into 5mm (¼in) pieces
4 garlic cloves, peeled and sliced
thumb-sized piece of fresh root ginger, peeled and finely grated
2 star anise
150ml (5fl oz/scant ⅔ cup) white wine of choice
fine sea salt and freshly ground black pepper

Pat the pork dry with kitchen paper and, using a sharp knife, score lines into the skin at 1cm (½in) intervals, taking care not to cut beyond the fat layer. Your butcher can do this for you if you prefer.

Rub 1 teaspoon of fine sea salt all over the pork joint and leave at room temperature for 15 minutes. This will help to give you crunchy crackling.

Preheat the air fryer to 200°C (400°F).

Mix the remaining ingredients together in a bowl. Pour them into the bottom of the air fryer along with a good pinch of salt and some black pepper.

Pat the pork dry again and sprinkle a little more salt over the skin, then place it on top of the vegetables and wine, skin-side up, and roast for 30 minutes. Reduce the temperature to 180°C (350°F) and roast for another hour.

Remove the pork and set aside to rest for 15 minutes. Return the vegetables to the air fryer and roast for a further 15 minutes.

When you are ready to eat, discard the star anise, then serve the vegetables alongside thick slices of pork and crackling. This recipe works well with mashed potatoes and simply steamed green vegetables.

Serves 4
–
Prep 30 mins
–
Cook 1 hr 45 mins

WHOLE ROAST CHICKEN WITH ORANGE & CORIANDER

Air fryers are fantastic for roasting large pieces of meat, and a whole chicken is no exception. I find it takes about 15 minutes less cooking time than in an oven, but always make sure you check that the chicken is cooked before serving – you can do this either with a meat thermometer or using the method below. This would be lovely served up with the sweet potato wedges on page 99 and the Tomato Salsa on page 119.

2 oranges: finely grated zest and juice of 1 (reserve the skins) and the other sliced into 5mm (¼in) rounds
4 garlic cloves, crushed
1 tbsp olive oil
1 tsp brown rice miso paste
2 tbsp ground coriander
1.6kg (3lb 8oz) whole chicken
1 red onion, thickly sliced
small bunch of fresh coriander (cilantro), leaves finely chopped and stalks reserved
sea salt and freshly ground black pepper

In a bowl, mix together the orange zest and juice, crushed garlic, olive oil, brown rice miso, ground coriander and some salt and pepper.

Stuff the chicken cavity with the reserved orange skins, half the red onion and all the coriander (cilantro) stalks.

Carefully pour the marinade over the chicken and rub it into the skin and all the crevices.

Leave to marinate in the fridge for a couple of hours, or overnight if possible, but don't worry if you don't have time.

Preheat the air fryer to 180°C (350°F).

Place the orange slices and remaining red onion slices onto the bottom of the basket, then place the whole chicken, breast-side up, on top. Air-fry for 1 hour, then pierce the thickest part of the thigh (just next to the breast) with a sharp knife and check the juices are clear. If you are feeling brave, you can also keep the knife inserted, count to 10, then touch the flat tip against the inside of your wrist. If it is too hot to hold for more than a fraction of a second, then the chicken is cooked!

Remove the chicken and leave to rest under a clean tea towel for 20 minutes.

Serve with the chopped coriander (cilantro) scattered over the top and drizzle over any cooking juices which have collected in the bottom of the air fryer.

Serves 4

–

Prep 20 mins, plus marinating

–

Cook 1 hr

Mains

NOT QUITE A CORNISH PASTY

I have swapped traditional swede (rutabaga) for carrots in this recipe, as I prefer the flavour, but do use swede if you like. You will need a food processor for this recipe, and the pasties are made in two batches (or bake them simultaneously if you have a two-drawer air fryer). I've used rump steak here, which cooks quickly and is tender but still with some good fat running through it.

For the pastry
350g (12oz) plain (all-purpose) flour, plus extra for dusting
85g (3oz) lard, cubed
85g (3oz) cold unsalted butter, cubed
pinch of salt
120ml (4fl oz/½ cup) cold water
olive oil, for brushing

For the filling
350g (12oz) rump steak, cut into 1cm (½in) pieces
100g (3½oz) carrots, peeled and cut into 5mm (¼in) dice
200g (7oz) potatoes, peeled and cut into 5mm (¼in) dice
1 small onion, finely chopped
1 tsp dried thyme
½ tsp smoked paprika
sea salt and freshly ground black pepper

To make the pastry, put the flour, lard and butter into a food processor along with a generous pinch of salt. Blitz until it resembles fine breadcrumbs, then, with the motor running, slowly pour in the cold water. Once it comes together in a ball, stop the motor and tip out onto a floured work surface. Gently squeeze into a round with your hands, wrap in some baking parchment or foil and put in the fridge for 15 minutes.

To make the filling, mix together the steak, carrots, potatoes, onion, dried thyme and paprika. Season well with salt and lots of black pepper.

Preheat the air fryer to 160°C (325°F).

Remove the pastry from the fridge and roll it out to about 4mm (¼in) thick. Cut into four 20cm (8in) circles (you can use a side plate as a guide).

Fill the centre of each circle with the meat mixture, leaving a 2cm (¾in) border. Brush some cold water around the border and fold in half, pressing down the edges to seal. Starting on one side, pinch and twist up the border to make a pasty shape, then snip 2–3 air holes in the top.

Place into the air fryer on a perforated liner, then brush with olive oil. Bake two at a time for 40 minutes. Chill the remaining pasties in the fridge while the others are cooking.

Remove and leave to cool for 20 minutes before tucking in!

Serves 4
–
Prep 20 mins
–
Cook 1 hr 20 mins

LAMB STEAKS WITH CORIANDER, CHILLI & LIME

Cooking on a high heat means the outside of the lamb caramelizes a little while the inside remains juicy and tender. This recipe works well with the air-fried potatoes on page 108 and the tomato salsa on page 119. If you have a double-drawer air fryer, you can cook both the lamb and the potatoes at the same time.

500g (1lb 2oz) lamb steaks, about 2cm (¾in) thick
3 spring onions (scallions), finely chopped
1 red chilli, deseeded and finely chopped
15g (½oz) fresh coriander (cilantro), finely chopped
juice of 1 lime
2 garlic cloves, finely chopped
1 tbsp extra virgin olive oil
sea salt and freshly ground black pepper

Preheat the air fryer to 200°C (400°F).

Cut the lamb into 2cm (¾in) thick strips and mix with the remaining ingredients, ensuring the lamb is well covered. Season well with salt and black pepper.

Tip everything into the air fryer and cook for 10 minutes.

Remove and serve immediately.

Serves 2
–
Prep 10 mins
–
Cook 10 mins

Mains

BAKED POTATOES WITH SMOKED SALMON & CREAM CHEESE

I love a baked potato, and these are ready much more quickly than in an oven, not to mention the reduced energy consumption. The filling possibilities are endless, but I've gone for a classic here. You could swap the smoked salmon and cream cheese for canned tuna, sweetcorn and sour cream or pile on the butter and Cheddar.

2 × 300g (10½oz) baking potatoes
1 tsp olive oil
4 tbsp cream cheese
1 lemon, cut in half
4 slices of smoked salmon
small bunch of chives, finely chopped
sea salt and freshly ground black
　　pepper

Preheat the air fryer to 190°C (375°F).

Prick the potatoes all over, then drizzle the olive oil over the skin and rub in a little sea salt.

Cook for 50 minutes.

Cut the potatoes in half, then scoop out the insides and transfer to a bowl. Mash with the cream cheese, a squeeze of lemon juice and a good pinch of salt. Spoon the mashed potatoes back into the crispy skins.

Top with the smoked salmon slices, squeeze over some more lemon juice and sprinkle on a few chives.

A good grind of black pepper finishes this dish off perfectly!

Serves 2
–
Prep 5 mins
–
Cook 50 mins

SPANISH CHICKEN THIGHS

A great midweek meal, since it takes such a short time to prepare. The chicken skin crisps up nicely, but the thighs are juicy and tender. This has become a favourite recipe in our house and would work well alongside the potato rösti on page 114. This recipe is best made in a basket air fryer, but you could also cook it in an ovenproof dish in an oven-style air fryer.

4 large chicken thighs, skin on
50g (1¾oz) cooking chorizo, cut into
  5mm (¼in) slices
1 red onion, peeled and cut into
  wedges
1 red (bell) pepper, deseeded and cut
  into 1cm (½in) strips
4 garlic cloves, thickly sliced
2 tsp rosemary, finely chopped
pinch of saffron, soaked in 1 tsp boiling
  water
1 tsp smoked paprika
1 tbsp extra virgin olive oil
sea salt and freshly ground black
  pepper
lemon wedges, to serve

Preheat the air fryer to 200°C (400°F).

In a large bowl, mix all of the ingredients together, ensuring the chicken is well coated in the herbs and spices. Season well with salt and pepper.

Tip the chorizo and vegetables into the basket of the air fryer, then place the chicken thighs, skin-side up, on top.

Cook for 20 minutes until the skin is crispy and the chicken is cooked through. Check the juices run clear when the chicken is pierced with a sharp knife.

Serve with lemon wedges for squeezing over.

Serves 2
–
Prep 10 mins
–
Cook 20 mins

SPINACH, FETA, PEA & FILO PIE

Here is my version of a classic filo pie but cooked in an air fryer. You won't need to add salt, as both the feta and Parmesan are already very salty. You'll need a sandwich tin which fits your air fryer to cook this in – I used a 20cm (8in) tin.

200g (7oz) baby leaf spinach
200g (7oz) feta, crumbled
2 large eggs, beaten
100g (3½oz) frozen peas, defrosted
35g (1¼oz) Parmesan, grated
4 large sheets of filo pastry, about
    45 × 25cm (17¾ x 10in)
80ml (2½fl oz/⅓ cup) olive oil,
    for brushing
freshly ground black pepper

Boil a kettle and cover the spinach with boiling water. Leave to wilt while you prepare the rest of the filling.

In a large bowl, mix together the feta, eggs, defrosted peas, Parmesan and some black pepper.

Drain the spinach and squeeze out as much moisture as you can. You want it to be as dry as possible, so squeeze hard!

Roughly chop the spinach and add to the egg mixture, giving it a good mix.

Preheat the air fryer to 180°C (350°F).

Brush both sides of each sheet of filo pastry with olive oil and lay them on top of each other.

Gently press the pastry into a 20cm (8in) round baking tin.

Spoon the filling into the middle, then fold the overhanging pastry on top and press down to seal in the filling.

Bake in the air fryer for 15 minutes until golden brown on top and set inside. Leave to cool for a few minutes before turning out and cutting into wedges.

Serves 2
–
Prep 15 mins
–
Cook 15 mins

SQUASH PASTA SAUCE VO

A nifty little recipe which produces a silky smooth sauce. You could fry up some chorizo to add some crunch if you like. Serve with any shape of pasta you like – I love to use conchiglie or orecchiette. You can also use a small butternut squash for this if you can't find an onion squash – since it's thicker you'll need to air-fry it for 45 minutes and add 1–2 tablespoons of pasta cooking water to the squash purée to loosen it.

1 onion squash (approx. 600g/1lb 5oz)
1 tbsp extra virgin olive oil, plus extra for drizzling
2 banana shallots, cut into large chunks
2 garlic cloves, peeled
sea salt and freshly ground black pepper

To serve
pasta of choice
grated Parmesan, or vegan alternative
a few thyme sprigs, leaves picked

Preheat the air fryer to 180°C (350°F).

Cut the squash in half and remove the seeds. Season the flesh with salt and pepper and drizzle with a little olive oil.

Put the shallots and garlic into the air fryer in 2 little mounds. Place the squash halves, cut-side down, on top, so the onion and garlic are tucked inside the squash cavity. This will prevent them from burning.

Cook for 35 minutes until the squash skin is blistered and the flesh is soft. Remove the squash, onion and garlic from the air fryer and set aside for 5 minutes until the squash is cool enough to handle.

Meanwhile, cook the pasta according to the packet instructions.

Peel away the skin from the squash, then transfer the squash flesh, shallots and garlic to a bowl along with the 1 tablespoon of extra virgin olive oil and a good pinch of salt and black pepper. Blitz with a stick blender until silky smooth.

Drain the pasta and return to the pan along with the squash sauce. Mix well to combine then serve scattered with some freshly grated Parmesan and thyme leaves.

Serves 2
–
Prep 5 mins
–
Cook 35 mins

QUICK FISH EN PAPILLOTE

I use foil for this as I find it easier to scrunch up, but you can also use baking parchment; just make sure there are no loose bits of paper which can catch on the cooking element.

1 small fennel bulb, finely sliced and
    fronds reserved to garnish
1 small carrot, peeled and cut into
    thin matchsticks
1 garlic clove, finely sliced
2.5cm (1in) piece of fresh root ginger,
    peeled and cut into thin matchsticks
1 red chilli, finely sliced
½ lemon, sliced
1 tbsp dark soy sauce
1 tsp toasted sesame oil
2 thick salmon fillets, skin on (approx.
    120–150g/4¼–5½oz each)
sea salt and freshly ground black

Preheat the air fryer to 190°C (375°F).

Lay out 2 large pieces of foil and put the vegetables, garlic, ginger, chilli and lemon slices into the middle. Toss briefly with your hands so everything is mixed together, then drizzle over the soy sauce and sesame oil.

Lay the salmon fillets on top of the vegetables and season well with salt and pepper.

Carefully bring up the sides of the foil and scrunch the tops together to make a parcel. Make sure you leave a small space at the top for the air to circulate inside the parcel.

Cook for 16 minutes.

Leave the parcels in the air fryer for 5 minutes to let the vegetables steam for a moment or two longer, then remove, scatter over the fennel fronds and serve immediately with some freshly boiled brown rice.

Serves 2
–
Prep 10 mins
–
Cook 16 mins

CHICKEN SCHNITZEL

This is a riff on the classic fried chicken dish but, made in an air fryer, it is much healthier, and you don't need to slave over a hot stove. Simply pop them in and get on with something else, like the coleslaw recipe on page 119! You could double this recipe, but you will need to cook the schnitzel in two batches and you will need two racks. If you can't get hold of matzo meal, use panko breadcrumbs instead.

2 skinless chicken breasts
3 tbsp plain (all-purpose) flour
1 egg, beaten with 1 tbsp cold water
50g (1¾oz) medium matzo meal
2 tbsp grated Parmesan
zest of 1 lemon; ½ lemon, cut into
    wedges, to serve
1 tbsp olive oil, plus extra for drizzling
olive oil cooking spray
sea salt and freshly ground black
    pepper

Layer the chicken breasts between 2 large pieces of greaseproof paper. Bash the chicken with a rolling pin, to flatten it out, until about 5mm (¼in) thick all over.

Place the flour, along with some salt and pepper, onto a plate. Pour the beaten egg into a wide bowl and, in a separate wide bowl, mix the matzo meal with the Parmesan, lemon zest, olive oil and some salt and pepper.

Dust each chicken breast in the flour, then dip into the egg and finally cover in the matzo crumb.

Preheat the air fryer to 180°C (350°F).

Place the chicken breasts into the air fryer, spray generously with cooking oil and cook for 15 minutes, turning it over halfway through.

Serve the schnitzel immediately with the lemon wedges and some coleslaw (see page 119).

Serves 2
–
Prep 20 mins
–
Cook 15 mins

MUSHROOM PITHIVIER v

This classic French dish is basically a big mushroom pie, and it looks impressive and tastes even better! A recipe for when you want to treat someone. There is a bit of advance hob cooking for the filling but nothing too strenuous. You can serve this alongside the broccoli with hazelnuts on page 106. You will need an air-fryer liner and a baking tin which fits your air fryer – I used a 20cm (8in) cake tin.

2 portobello mushrooms
1 tbsp olive oil, plus extra to drizzle
1 small onion, finely chopped
2 garlic cloves, finely chopped
200g (7oz) chestnut mushrooms, finely chopped
3–4 fresh thyme sprigs, leaves only
50g (1¾oz) walnuts, finely chopped
4 tbsp double (heavy) cream
½ tsp Dijon mustard
plain (all-purpose) flour, for dusting
1 × 320g (11¼oz) sheet ready-rolled all-butter puff pastry
1 small egg, beaten
sea salt and freshly ground black pepper

Preheat the air fryer to 200°C (400°F).

Place the portobello mushrooms into the air fryer, cup-side up, drizzle with a little oil and season well with salt and pepper. Roast for 8 minutes, then remove and set aside to cool.

Meanwhile, heat the 1 tablespoon of olive oil in a frying pan and fry the onion and garlic over a medium heat for 3–4 minutes until soft. Then add the chopped chestnut mushrooms and thyme leaves and fry for another 10 minutes until all the moisture has evaporated.

Season well with salt and pepper, then add the walnuts, double (heavy) cream and mustard. Let this bubble away for a couple of minutes until thick. Spread it out onto a cold plate to cool quickly.

Unroll the pastry onto a lightly floured work surface. Roll it a little larger so you can cut out 2 × 20cm (8in) circles.

Spread half the cooled mushroom mixture over one circle, leaving a 2cm (¾in) border. Top with the cooked portobello mushrooms, cup-side down, and top with the remaining mushroom mixture. Place the second circle over the top, pressing down the edges to seal the filling inside. Crimp the edges with a fork and, if you like, lightly score a pattern into the top using the tip of a knife.

Brush the top with the beaten egg and transfer to a round baking tin, lined with a parchment liner.

Bake at 200°C (400°F) for 22 minutes until the top is golden and puffed up.

Carefully remove from the air fryer and serve immediately.

Serves 2
–
Prep 25 mins
–
Cook 30 mins

WHOLE TIKKA MASALA CAULIFLOWER VE

A show-stopping, self-saucing vegan centrepiece. Simply boil some brown or wild rice which will cook in the same time it takes to make the cauliflower. This is best made in a basket air fryer without the rack, so the sauce and cauliflower cook on the base of the basket. If you don't have this type of air fryer, then make it in a roasting tin in your air fryer.

1 large cauliflower
2 tbsp olive oil
1 small red onion, finely diced
2 garlic cloves, grated
1 small thumb fresh root ginger, finely grated
1 tsp garam masala
1 tsp ground turmeric
½ tsp cayenne pepper
1 × 400g (14oz) can chopped tomatoes
50g (1¾oz) pine nuts
100ml (3½fl oz/scant ½ cup) coconut cream, or cream of your choice
small bunch of coriander (cilantro), roughly chopped
sea salt and freshly ground black pepper

Remove the large leaves from the cauliflower and discard. Cut off the smaller, tender leaves and set aside. Trim the bottom of the cauliflower so it sits flat.

Place the cauliflower head into a large saucepan, cover with water and bring to the boil. Simmer for 5 minutes, then drain and transfer to a large bowl.

Place the olive oil, red onion, garlic, ginger, garam masala, turmeric, cayenne and chopped tomatoes into a food processor and blitz until smooth.

Preheat the air fryer to 180°C (350°F).

Pour the marinade over the top of the cauliflower and turn it over so it is completely covered in the sauce.

Transfer the cauliflower to the air fryer, cut-side down and pour over the sauce. Air-fry for 30 minutes until slightly blackened on top.

Meanwhile, toast the pine nuts in a dry frying pan for 3–4 minutes until golden, then set aside.

After 30 minutes, tuck the reserved cauliflower leaves around the sides of the cauliflower, and air-fry for another 10 minutes.

To serve, carefully remove the cauliflower from the air fryer and transfer to a serving platter. Spoon over the sauce, then pour the coconut cream on top. Finally sprinkle over the chopped coriander (cilantro) and toasted pine nuts.

Serves 4
–
Prep 15 mins
–
Cook 50 mins

Mains

BLUE CHEESE CALZONE

Pre-made pizza dough makes this recipe so easy to pull together. You can, of course, make your own pizza dough if you have the time. Substitute pepperoni for the blue cheese if you prefer a meaty calzone. This can be made in a basket or oven-style air fryer, and both calzones can cook together if you have a double-drawer model.

1 × 400g (14oz) sheet pre-rolled pizza dough
4 tbsp passata
140g (5oz) grated mozzarella
40g (1½oz) blue cheese, such as Gorgonzola, Stilton or Saint Agur, crumbled

Preheat the air fryer to 200°C (400°F).

Cut the pizza dough in half to give you 2 squares or semicircles (this will depend on the shape of the pre-rolled pizza dough).

Spread 2 tablespoons of passata over each piece, leaving a 2cm (¾in) border. Sprinkle over the mozzarella and dot over the blue cheese. Fold the dough in half, enclosing the filling, creating either a triangle or a quadrant. Pinch the edges together and, starting on one side, pinch and twist up the border to make a pasty shape.

Snip 2 air holes in the top and bake the calzones one at a time (keep the first calzone warm under a clean tea towel while you bake the second one) for 9 minutes until golden brown and melting inside.

Serves 2
–
Prep 5 mins
–
Cook 18 mins

CRISPY SEA BASS WITH FENNEL & CAPER BUTTER

An incredibly quick supper which you could serve alongside the couscous on page 119 or the skin-on chunky chips on page 116. A whole lemon is used here with half for the fish and the other half used in the sauce.

1 fennel bulb, cut into 5mm (¼in) slices, fronds reserved for garnish
½ lemon, cut into slices
1 tbsp extra virgin olive oil, plus extra for brushing
2 × 120–150g (4¼–5½oz) sea bass fillets, skin on
sea salt and freshly ground black pepper

For the butter sauce
50g (1¾oz) unsalted butter
1 tbsp capers, rinsed
juice of ½ lemon
pinch of salt

Preheat the air fryer to 180°C (350°F).

Mix the fennel and lemon slices together with the tablespoon of olive oil and some salt and pepper.

Pat the fish skin dry, then brush both sides with a little olive oil and season with salt.

Place the fennel and lemon into the air fryer, then pop the fish, skin-side up, on top. Cook for 10 minutes until the skin is crispy and the fish is opaque.

Meanwhile, put the butter, capers, lemon juice and salt into a small saucepan and heat gently until the butter has melted. Set aside until the fish is ready.

Serve each fillet with half the fennel and lemon slices, then spoon over lots of buttery caper sauce and garnish with the reserved fennel fronds.

Serves 2
–
Prep 5 mins
–
Cook 10 mins

Mains

SPICED RACK OF LAMB

This is a real treat and takes almost no time to prepare. Ask your butcher to prepare the rack for you so the exposed bones are free of any excess fat. Serve with a green salad and the couscous on page 119 or the Air-fried Potato Slices with Za'atar on page 108.

1 tbsp harissa paste
2 tbsp Greek yogurt
1 tsp ground cumin
2 tsp ground coriander
1 tsp garlic granules
500g (1lb 2oz) organic or free-range rack of lamb, trimmed
sea salt and freshly ground black pepper

Mix together the harissa, yogurt, cumin, coriander and garlic granules along with a good pinch of salt and black pepper.

Score the fat side of the lamb in a diamond pattern and cover with the marinade, pressing it into all the nooks and crannies. Cover and leave at room temperature for 30 minutes.

Preheat the air fryer to 190°C (375°F).

Place the lamb rack into the air fryer, fat-side up, and cook for 12 minutes until crisp and brown.

Leave to rest inside the warm air fryer for 5 minutes, then serve, sliced into chops with some couscous and a leafy green salad.

Serves 4
–
Prep 10 mins, plus marinating
–
Cook 12 mins

CHICKEN THIGHS WITH CREAM, LEEKS & PEAS

This is a bit like a casserole but made in an air fryer. You can make this either directly on the bottom of your basket air fryer, or in an ovenproof dish which fits inside your air fryer – you want a container to retain the juices. You could serve this alongside the Lemon & Rosemary Roast Potatoes on page 100 or some mashed potato.

150ml (5fl oz/scant ⅔ cup) hot chicken stock
1 tbsp Dijon mustard
20g (¾oz) Parmesan, grated
1 leek, washed and finely sliced
4 × 150g (5½oz) chicken thighs, skin on
25g (1oz) unsalted butter
50ml (1¾fl oz/3½ tbsp) double (heavy) cream
100g (3½oz) frozen peas, defrosted
small bunch of flat-leaf parsley, finely chopped
sea salt and freshly ground black pepper

Preheat the air fryer to 190°C (375°F).

In a measuring jug (cup), mix together the hot chicken stock, mustard and Parmesan. Season well with salt and pepper.

Pour into the bottom of your air fryer along with the leek and stir to combine. Place the chicken thighs on top, skin-side up, and dot over the butter.

Roast for 30 minutes, then pour in the double (heavy) cream and defrosted peas. Try not to splash or cover the chicken skin, which will be nice and crispy by now. Give the basket a little shake so the peas and cream sink down into the sauce and air-fry for another 5 minutes.

Serve immediately and sprinkle with the chopped parsley.

Serves 2
–
Prep 5 mins
–
Cook 35 mins

SIDES

You'll find plenty of easy-to-prepare side dishes here, all of which go well with the recipes in the Mains chapter. Air fryers are best friends with potatoes of all kinds and you have plenty of options here, alongside some more interesting vegetable side dishes. The roast potatoes or chips are a great place to begin – and as an added bonus you'll feel smug about how little fat you'll use.

SWEET POTATO WEDGES VO

These are best made with long wedges as they look so beautiful once they are cooked. A doddle to prepare – they literally take 5 minutes. Lovely with the Garlic Yogurt on page 118 and served alongside the Whole Roast Chicken on page 67.

1kg (2lb 4oz) sweet potatoes, washed and cut into 2cm (¾in) wedges
1 tbsp olive oil
sea salt
Garlic Yogurt (page 118), to serve

Mix the sweet potato wedges with the olive oil and salt.

Preheat the air fryer to 190°C (375°F).

Roast for 25 minutes, shaking the basket halfway through, or turn the potatoes with tongs if using an oven-style air fryer.

Serve immediately with the garlic yogurt spooned over the top.

Serves 4
–
Prep 5 mins
–
Cook 25 mins

LEMON & ROSEMARY ROAST POTATOES

Air-fried roast potatoes are so much quicker than roasting them in the oven, and this recipe is great for small numbers. These work brilliantly alongside the Chicken Thighs with Cream, Leeks & Peas on page 94.

1.2kg (2lb 10oz) Maris Piper potatoes, peeled and cut into even-sized chunks
1 lemon
3 rosemary sprigs
good pinch of sea salt
1 heaped tbsp duck or goose fat

Put the potatoes into a large saucepan of cold water with thick strips of peel from half the lemon, a sprig of rosemary and the salt.

Cover with a lid and bring to the boil. Simmer for 5 minutes, then drain well, removing the lemon peel and rosemary.

Toss the potatoes in the duck or goose fat, ensuring each piece is well coated.

Preheat the air fryer to 200°C (400°F).

Tip in the potatoes and roast for 20 minutes, tossing halfway through cooking.

Meanwhile, finely grate the rest of the lemon and finely chop the needles from the remaining rosemary sprigs.

Sprinkle the lemon zest and rosemary over the potatoes, giving them a good mix, and return to the air fryer for another 5 minutes.

Serve immediately.

Serves 4
–
Prep 15 mins
–
Cook 25 mins

HONEY & SESAME ROAST PARSNIPS VO

This classic pairing of honey with sesame seeds to takes your roast parsnips to the next level. Speedy to prepare and even speedier to disappear into your mouth!

500g (1lb 2oz) parsnips, peeled and cut
    into 5cm (2in) batons
1 tbsp runny honey, agave syrup or
    maple syrup
1 tbsp sesame seeds
1 tbsp olive oil
sea salt

Preheat the air fryer to 180°C (350°F).

Mix the parsnips with the runny honey, sesame seeds, olive oil and a good pinch of salt.

Air-fry for 18 minutes, shaking the basket halfway through.

Serve immediately.

Serves 4
–
Prep 5 mins
–
Cook 18 mins

GARLIC & NIGELLA SEED TEAR & SHARE BREAD VG

Using the dehydrator part of your air fryer is a little like using a proving oven and gives you consistent results. Soft and chewy in the middle and crunchy on the top, this bread is delicious on its own but also great served with the chicken thighs on page 94. You will need a 20cm (8in) cake tin.

300g (10½oz) strong white bread flour, plus extra for dusting
1 tsp fast action yeast
1 tsp salt
1 tsp garlic powder
2 tsp nigella seeds
100ml (3½fl oz/scant ½ cup) milk of your choice
120ml (4fl oz/½ cup) lukewarm water
1 tbsp olive oil, plus extra for greasing
2 garlic cloves, finely chopped

Mix together the flour, yeast, salt, garlic powder and half the nigella seeds. Pour in the milk and water and mix to form a rough dough.

Turn out onto a lightly floured work surface and knead for 10–15 minutes until smooth and elastic (or 8–10 minutes in a stand mixer using a dough hook). Form into a ball and place in a greased 20cm (8in) cake tin, then cover the tin with foil.

Set the air fryer to 40°C (105°F). Pop the tin into the air fryer and prove the dough for 1 hour or until doubled in size.

Turn the dough out onto a lightly floured surface and cut into 6 equal pieces. Form each one into a smooth ball and place them, spaced apart, back into the baking tin. Cover with foil, return to the air fryer and prove again for 45 minutes–1 hour until almost doubled in size.

Mix the remaining 1 teaspoon of nigella seeds with the olive oil and chopped garlic.

Remove the dough balls and preheat the air fryer to 200°C (400°F).

Brush the rolls with the olive oil and garlic mixture. Air-fry for 10 minutes, then reduce the heat to 180°C (350°F) and air-fry for another 15 minutes. Carefully remove the bread from the tin, turn upside down and return to the air fryer (upside down) for another 10 minutes.

Remove and serve with lots of butter.

Serves 4
–
Prep 25 mins,
2 hrs proving
–
Cook 35 mins

Sides

BROCCOLI WITH HAZELNUTS & CHILLI

A lovely way to eat your greens – the broccoli retains some bite and the hazelnuts work beautifully alongside the green florets. This recipe uses up the broccoli stalks so there is no waste – just chop them up and roast them alongside the florets. They take a little longer to cook, so make sure they are cut smaller than the florets. I would eat this alongside the Mushroom Pithivier on page 84. You can omit the chilli if heat isn't your thing.

1 broccoli head, cut into florets and stalk cut into batons
50g (1¾oz) hazelnuts, roughly chopped
1 red chilli, deseeded and finely chopped
4 tbsp olive oil
sea salt and freshly ground black pepper
20g (1¾oz) Parmesan flakes or shavings, to serve

Preheat the air fryer to 190°C (375°F).

In a large bowl, mix the broccoli with the hazelnuts, chilli, olive oil and some salt and pepper, ensuring all the florets and stalks are covered.

Transfer to the air fryer and roast for 7 minutes until the broccoli is tender and beginning to char.

Serve with the Parmesan flakes over the top.

Serves 2
–
Prep 10 mins
–
Cook 7 mins

AIR-FRIED POTATO SLICES WITH ZA'ATAR VE

This recipe came about when I was in more of a hurry than usual to make dinner. I had potatoes that needed using up and really wanted fried potatoes without the faff of watching them in the pan with my small kids running around. These are ideal with a fried egg on top.

500g (1lb 2oz) Maris Piper potatoes, washed and sliced into 3mm (⅛in) rounds
cooking oil spray
sea salt
1 tsp za'atar

Preheat the air fryer to 200°C (400°F).

Soak the potato slices in cold water for 5 minutes (to get rid of any excess starch), then drain and pat dry.

Place into the air-fryer basket and spray liberally with oil. Sprinkle with sea salt and air-fry for 20 minutes, shaking the basket halfway through (or turn the slices over if using an oven-style air fryer) so all the potatoes cook evenly. Sprinkle over the za'atar and cook for another 2 minutes.

Remove and serve immediately.

Serves 2
–
Prep 5 mins
–
Cook 22 mins

BRUSSELS SPROUTS WITH PANCETTA & COMTÉ

Green brassicas cook brilliantly in an air fryer so you could substitute shredded cavolo nero or curly kale for the Brussels sprouts here; just reduce the cooking time to 6 minutes in total. A decadent side, as the Comté melts on top of the warm sprouts.

500g (1lb 2oz) Brussels sprouts, washed, trimmed and halved
100g (3½oz) unsmoked pancetta cubes
olive oil, for drizzling
100g (3½oz) cooked chestnuts, crumbled
40g (1½oz) Comté, grated
sea salt and freshly ground black pepper

Preheat the air fryer to 180°C (350°F).

Mix together the Brussels sprouts, pancetta, a light drizzle of olive oil and some salt and black pepper.

Tip into the air fryer and roast for 10 minutes, shaking the basket halfway through.

Add the chestnuts and cook for another 2 minutes.

Serve immediately with the Comté sprinkled over the top.

Serves 4
–
Prep 5 mins
–
Cook 12 mins

SLOW-ROASTED TOMATOES VE

These sticky, squashy tomatoes work perfectly on toast with some ricotta or cream cheese. They are a fridge essential for when you need to pull together a fast working lunch and are lovely alongside The Ultimate Cheese Toastie on page 58. This works in either style of air fryer but you will need two racks.

8 plum tomatoes, halved
1 tsp sea salt
2 tbsp best-quality balsamic vinegar
freshly ground black pepper
1 tbsp olive oil

Mix the tomato halves with the salt, balsamic vinegar, a good grinding of black pepper and the olive oil.

Place, cut-side up, into a roasting tin that fits your air fryer (you can also cook these directly in the basket or shelf of your air fryer).

Cook at 160°C (325°F) for 1 hour until the tomatoes are soft and squishy. Store any leftovers in an airtight container in the fridge for 2–3 days.

Serves 4
–
Prep 5 mins
–
Cook 1 hr

GIANT POTATO RÖSTI v

A bit like a giant potato cake, this rösti works nicely alongside the Whole Roast Chicken with Orange & Coriander on page 67. Or you could go all out and serve it with a dollop of sour cream and some smoked salmon or lumpfish caviar.

800g (1lb 12oz) Maris Piper potatoes, washed and coarsely grated
2 tbsp olive oil
4 thyme sprigs, leaves only
1 large egg, beaten
2 tbsp plain (all-purpose) flour
25g (1oz) unsalted butter
sea salt

Preheat the air fryer to 190°C (375°F).

Place the grated potatoes into a clean piece of muslin (cheesecloth) or tea towel and squeeze out as much liquid as you can.

Transfer the potatoes to a bowl and mix well with the olive oil, thyme leaves, beaten egg and flour and a good pinch of salt; I like to use my hands for this.

Line the air fryer with a perforated sheet of parchment, then tip the potato mixture in, pressing down firmly in an even layer so it spreads out and fills the whole basket.

Bake for 15 minutes, then dot over the butter and bake for a further 10 minutes until the top is golden and crispy.

Carefully remove the rösti, flip it over and return to the air fryer to cook the other side for another 10 minutes.

Serves 4
–
Prep 15 mins
–
Cook 35 mins

SKIN-ON CHUNKY CHIPS VE

If you fancy fish and chips, then these work nicely with the Crispy Sea Bass on page 91 or the Quick Fish en Papillote on page 80. You could also serve these as a snack with either of the mayonnaise recipes on page 118. Make the mayo while the chips are cooking.

2 × 300g (10½oz) King Edward or Rooster potatoes, washed
1 tsp dried rosemary
1 tbsp olive oil
1 tsp sea salt

Cut the potatoes into 1cm (½in) thick chips and place into a large heatproof bowl.

Fill and boil a kettle. Cover the potatoes with just-boiled water and set aside for 10 minutes – this is a bit like par-boiling but much easier!

Preheat the air fryer to 190°C (375°F).

Drain the potatoes and pat dry with some kitchen paper or a clean tea towel.

Mix the potatoes with the rosemary, olive oil and sea salt, ensuring all the chips are well coated.

Tip into the air fryer and air-fry for 25 minutes, shaking the basket 3 times during cooking to ensure they cook evenly.

Serves 2
–
Prep 15 mins
–
Cook 25 mins

DUKKAH VE

A useful little mix to have in your store cupboard. It will work with the dips on pages 18 and 30, the roast chicken on page 67, the lamb steaks on page 71 and even a poached egg!

Makes 100g (3½oz)
1 tbsp cumin seeds
1 tbsp coriander seeds
1 tbsp fennel seeds
2 tbsp sesame seeds
2 tbsp flaked (slivered) almonds

Toast all the ingredients in a dry frying pan for 3–4 minutes, stirring regularly until the almonds have turned golden brown. Store in an airtight container for up to a month.

SINGLE EGG YOLK MAYONNAISE V

You won't ever regret making your own mayonnaise – it is faster than nipping down to the shops to buy the pre-made stuff!

Makes 150ml (5fl oz/scant ²/₃ cup)
1 large organic egg yolk
½ tsp English mustard powder
½ tsp sea salt
pinch of freshly ground black pepper
1 tsp white wine vinegar or lemon juice
120ml (4fl oz/½ cup) light olive oil or sunflower oil
small handful of freshly chopped herbs, such as fennel, flat-leaf parsley and chives (optional)

Place a small glass bowl onto a tea towel (to prevent it from moving around), then, using a hand-held electric whisk, whisk together the egg yolk, mustard powder, salt, pepper and white wine vinegar until combined. Keep whisking and slowly pour in the oil until you have a thick sauce. You want a steady stream of oil – about 1mm thick. Stir in the herbs, if using.

Keep for up to 3 days in an airtight container in the fridge.

If you add the oil too quickly, the mayonnaise will split. If this happens, start again with another egg yolk in the bowl and slowly pour the split mixture in, again in a very slow and steady stream, followed by any remaining oil and an additional 100ml (3½fl oz/scant ½ cup) light olive oil.

VEGAN MAYONNAISE VE

A fast, easy and fuss-free alternative to the mayo above.

Makes 350g (12oz)
300g (10½oz) block silken tofu, drained
1 tsp Dijon mustard
1 tbsp lemon juice, white wine vinegar or apple cider vinegar
2 tbsp extra virgin olive oil
1 tsp sea salt
freshly ground black pepper

Using a stick blender, blitz all the ingredients together until you have a smooth, thick sauce. Store in an airtight container in the fridge for up to a week.

GARLIC YOGURT WITH SUMAC V

An easy-to-make accompaniment which sits well in a mezze platter or dolloped on the side of some fries.

Serves 4
200g (7oz) plain yogurt
1 garlic clove, finely grated
juice of ½ lemon
1 tbsp extra virgin olive oil
pinch of sea salt
½ tsp sumac

Mix all the ingredients apart from the sumac together, then sprinkle over the sumac to finish.

COLESLAW VO

Serves 2
¼ small red cabbage, finely shredded
¼ small Savoy cabbage, finely shredded
1 medium carrot, peeled and grated
2 spring onions (scallions), finely chopped
small handful of fresh mint leaves and
   coriander (cilantro), roughly chopped
1 tbsp wholegrain mustard
4 tsp mayonnaise of your choice
juice of ½ lemon
sea salt and freshly ground black pepper

If you have a food processor you can make this really quickly by using the grating and slicing attachments. Delicious on the side of the cheese toastie on page 58 or alongside the Blue Cheese Calzone on page 88.

Mix all the ingredients together.

It will keep for up to 2 days in the fridge but is best eaten on the day it's made.

TOMATO SALSA VE

Serves 2
200g (7oz) cherry tomatoes, quartered
½ red onion, finely chopped
1 tbsp extra virgin olive oil
1 green chilli, deseeded and finely
   chopped
1 tbsp red wine vinegar
sea salt and freshly ground black pepper

This is a quick little salad which peps up any number of the dishes in the Mains chapter. You could add some freshly chopped herbs if you like – chives would go nicely, as would mint.

Mix all the ingredients together and season well with salt and black pepper.

COUSCOUS VE

Serves 4
2 tsp vegetable bouillon
300ml (10½fl oz/1¼ cups + 1 tbsp) boiling
   water
150g (5½oz) couscous
a drizzle of extra virgin olive oil
small bunch of fresh dill, parsley and
   mint, finely chopped
sea salt and freshly ground black pepper

Super quick and easy to prepare and made in a couple of minutes, this is a great alternative to rice. All you have to do it wait for the couscous to steam.

Mix the vegetable bouillon with the boiling water. Pour over the couscous, season well with salt and pepper and cover with a plate or cling film (plastic wrap). Leave the couscous to steam for 10 minutes, then drizzle over some olive oil, stir in the chopped herbs and serve.

SWEET THINGS

Here you have lots of easy recipes which cover breakfast, pudding and afternoon tea. Some are super-fast like the granola and raspberry cupcakes, and some are best for weekend cooking when you can be a little more leisurely, like the Sweet Cardamom Bread Rolls or the Almond Meringues.

RASPBERRY CUPCAKES

Small batch baking works well in an air fryer and means you have a naughty treat in no time at all. These cupcakes are best made using silicone cupcake cases or a cupcake mould which fits your air fryer.

65g (2¼oz) self-raising (self-rising) flour, sifted
65g (2¼oz) caster (superfine) sugar
1 large egg
65g (2¼oz) very soft unsalted butter
1 tsp vanilla bean paste
12 fresh raspberries, to decorate

For the icing
200g (7oz) full-fat cream cheese
2 tbsp icing (confectioners') sugar, sifted
1 tbsp raspberry jam
½ tsp vanilla bean paste

Preheat the air fryer to 160°C (325°F).

In a bowl, stir together the flour and sugar. Crack in the egg, then add the butter and vanilla bean paste and, using a hand-held electric whisk, beat until smooth and combined.

Spoon the batter into the silicone cupcake cases and carefully place in the air fryer. Bake for 13 minutes until golden, then set aside to cool.

Meanwhile, make the icing by gently folding together the cream cheese, icing (confectioners') sugar, raspberry jam and vanilla bean paste. Don't overmix or the cream cheese will become runny. Refrigerate until the cakes are cool enough to ice.

Spread the icing over the top of each cake and decorate with the raspberries. Best enjoyed immediately.

Makes 6
–
Prep 10 mins
–
Cook 13 mins

GIANT PEANUT BUTTER & CHOCOLATE CHIP COOKIES

Crisp on top and gooey in the middle, there is nothing nicer than freshly baked cookies. Making individual ones can be a bit of a faff, so I've made giant ones here which you cut into wedges to serve. I would serve this as a pudding rather than as a snack. You can make the dough ahead and refrigerate it, then bake the cookies to order.

60g (2¼oz) crunchy peanut butter
75g (2½oz) unsalted butter
90g (3¼oz) light soft brown sugar
1 large egg
110g (3¾oz) self-raising (self-rising) flour, sifted
90g (3¼oz) dark chocolate chips
sea salt

In a saucepan, melt together the peanut butter and butter. Stir well to combine.

In a large bowl, mix the melted butters with the sugar, using a wooden spoon, then crack in the egg and mix again.

Add the flour, chocolate chips and a pinch of salt, then mix briefly until you have a very soft mixture.

Preheat the air fryer to 190°C (375°F).

Line the air fryer with a sheet of perforated baking parchment and spoon half the mixture on top. Flatten it down with a spatula, spreading the mixture out to make a 20cm (8in) cookie.

Bake for 10 minutes, then carefully remove from the air fryer and repeat with the remaining dough.

Cut each cookie into quarters and serve with some vanilla ice cream. Any leftovers will keep in an airtight container for a couple of days.

Serves 8

–

Prep 10 mins

–

Cook 20 mins

ORANGE & PEANUT BUTTER FRENCH TOAST

A delightful recipe which works beautifully for breakfast or brunch. You could use any type of nut butter for this and, if you are feeling decadent, you could serve this with a drizzle of maple syrup or a sprinkling of icing (confectioners') sugar. You'll need a perforated air-fryer liner for this to prevent the bread from sticking.

1 egg, beaten
100ml (3½fl oz/scant ½ cup) milk
    of your choice
¼ tsp vanilla extract
½ tsp mixed spice
zest of 1 orange (reserve the segments
    to serve)
4 slices of white bread
soft unsalted butter
smooth peanut butter
2 tsp soft dark brown sugar

Preheat the air fryer to 200°C (400°F).

In a large bowl, whisk together the egg, milk, vanilla extract, mixed spice and orange zest. Set aside while you make the sandwiches.

Take 2 slices of bread, and butter both sides of each slice. Spread one slice with peanut butter and sprinkle over 1 teaspoon of the soft brown sugar. Top with the second slice of bread. Repeat with the remaining slices to make the second sandwich.

Cut each sandwich in half diagonally, then dip into the egg mixture. Press the sandwiches down to soak up as much of the batter as possible.

Carefully place the sandwiches, in a single layer, onto a perforated air-fryer liner, then place into the air fryer and cook for 6 minutes until puffed up and golden brown. Depending on the size of your air fryer, you may need to cook one sandwich at a time.

Serve immediately with the reserved orange segments.

Serves 2
–
Prep 4 mins
–
Cook 6 mins

COCONUT BANANA FRITTERS

My inspiration for this dish came from the deep-fried banana fritters we used to get as children with our Chinese takeaway. I also wanted to use the well-known combination of coconut, banana and strawberry and this is what I came up with. These work nicely as a breakfast or as a naughty pudding. Warm and fudgy in the middle and crisp on the outside, these fritters can be made in any air fryer.

2 bananas, peeled
30g (1oz) plain (all-purpose) flour
1 tsp mixed spice
1 tbsp light or dark soft brown sugar
1 small egg, beaten
60g (2¼oz) desiccated coconut
1 tbsp melted coconut oil or olive oil

To serve
maple syrup
a few fresh strawberries, sliced

Cut the bananas in half lengthways.

Arrange 3 bowls. Mix the flour, mixed spice and brown sugar in one. Put the beaten egg into the second and mix the desiccated coconut and melted coconut (or olive) oil together in the third.

Preheat the air fryer to 200°C (400°F).

Dip the banana pieces into the flour, then the egg and finally the desiccated coconut until they have all been covered.

Carefully place into the hot air fryer and fry for 4 minutes, then carefully turn over and fry for a further 2 minutes until crispy and golden.

Serve with maple syrup poured over the top and some sliced strawberries.

Serves 2
–
Prep 5 mins
–
Cook 6 mins

LEMON & VANILLA SCONES

This is super quick and requires a food processor for speed. You can always make the scones in the traditional way, by hand, if you don't have a food processor. You will need a perforated air-fryer liner for this recipe along with a 6cm (2½in) cookie cutter or water glass.

225g (8oz) plain (all-purpose) flour, plus extra for dusting
1 tsp baking powder
30g (1oz) ground almonds
2 tbsp caster (superfine) sugar
finely grated zest of 1 lemon
60g (2¼oz) cold unsalted butter, cubed
1 large egg
1 tsp vanilla bean paste
100ml (3½fl oz/scant ½ cup) whole milk, plus extra for brushing

To serve
lemon curd
crème fraîche

Preheat the air fryer to 180°C (350°F).

Place the flour, baking powder, ground almonds, sugar and lemon zest into a food processor and pulse until everything is mixed together. Add the butter and blitz again until the mixture resembles fine breadcrumbs.

Tip the mixture into a large mixing bowl. Beat together the egg and vanilla bean paste, then pour into the dry ingredients along with the milk. Mix with a wooden spoon to combine into a soft dough. It will be sticky but don't worry!

Tip the mixture out onto a floured work surface and gently pat and knead to bring the dough together. Press into a disc about 2cm (¾in) thick and cut out 6 scones.

Line the air fryer with parchment and place the scones into the basket, spaced apart. Brush with a little milk and bake for 15 minutes.

Remove and once cool enough to handle, cut in half and serve with some lemon curd and crème fraîche.

These will keep for a couple of days in an airtight container, if they last that long!

Makes 6
–
Prep 10 mins
–
Cook 15 mins

APRICOT CUSTARD PUFFS

I have a weakness for custard and, while developing this recipe, I discovered that Bird's custard powder can be made into a version of crème pâtissière, which is what you'll find in shop-bought pastries. You'll need an air-fryer liner to stop the pastry from sticking here.

140ml (4½fl oz/generous ½ cup) whole milk, plus 1 tbsp for brushing
3 tsp caster (superfine) sugar
3 heaped tsp custard powder
1 × 320g (11¼oz) sheet of ready-rolled all-butter puff pastry
8 tsp apricot jam
8 canned apricot halves or 4 canned peach halves, cut in half
icing (confectioners') sugar, for dusting

Mix together the milk, sugar and custard powder in a saucepan.

Place over a medium heat and bring to the boil, whisking continuously until thickened. Spread out onto a large plate to cool quickly.

Unroll the pastry and cut into 8 rectangles.

Spread 1 teaspoon of apricot jam over each rectangle, leaving a 1.5cm (⅝in) border.

Divide the cooled custard between the rectangles, spooning it on top of the jam. Top each one with an apricot half or half a canned peach.

Preheat the air fryer to 180°C (350°F).

Pinch together the opposite corners of each square to make little parcels and place 4 pastries at a time into your air fryer, lined with parchment. Brush each pastry with a little milk and bake for 15 minutes. Set aside while you bake the remaining pastries.

Once cool, dust with some sifted icing (confectioners') sugar. Best eaten on the day they are made, preferably as soon as they are out of the air fryer.

> Makes 8
> –
> Prep 15 mins
> –
> Cook 30 mins

Sweet Things

BANANA GRANOLA VE

This is a great way of using up a banana which is past its best. Best served with plain yogurt and plenty of fresh fruit. You will need a cake tin liner for this – or a shallow tray which fits inside your air fryer.

100g (3½oz) whole oats
50g (1¾oz) blanched hazelnuts, roughly chopped
50g (1¾oz) flaked (slivered) almonds
1 tsp mixed spice
1 banana
2 tbsp maple syrup
3 tbsp light olive oil
handful of sultanas, raisins or chopped dried apricots

Preheat the air fryer to 180°C (350°F).

In a bowl, stir together the oats, hazelnuts, almonds and mixed spice.

In a separate bowl, mash the banana with the maple syrup and olive oil, then stir into the oats.

Spread the mixture in a thin layer onto an air-fryer liner and bake for 12 minutes, stirring halfway through.

Remove and mix in the dried fruit.

Store in an airtight container for up to 2 weeks.

Serves 2
–
Prep 2 mins
–
Cook 12 mins

Sweet Things

SWEET CARDAMOM BREAD ROLLS

These rolls are a mixture between Finnish pulla bread and Swedish cardamom buns. Made into rolls, they cook quickly and are fun to tear apart. Delicious the following day, but I doubt they will last that long! You will need a deep, round baking tin or a deep non-stick baking dish which fits inside your air fryer.

125ml (4fl oz/½ cup) whole milk, plus extra for brushing
50g (1¾oz) soft unsalted butter
50g (1¾oz) light soft brown sugar, plus 2 tbsp
½ tsp vanilla bean paste or extract
16 cardamom pods, crushed
350g (12oz) strong white bread flour, plus extra for dusting
5g (¹/₈oz) fast action yeast
1 large egg
sunflower or vegetable oil, for greasing

Gently heat the milk, butter, 50g (1¾oz) sugar, vanilla bean paste and 10 cardamom pods in a small saucepan just until the butter has melted, then set aside to cool. Do not overheat it or the liquid will be too hot and will kill the yeast.

Remove the seeds from the remaining 6 cardamom pods and finely crush them in a pestle and mortar.

Mix the crushed cardamom seeds with the flour and yeast, make a well in the centre and crack in the egg. Once the milk has cooled to tepid, strain it into a jug to remove the cardamom pods. Pour the milk onto the flour and egg, then mix together to form a soft dough.

Turn out onto a lightly floured work surface and knead for 10–15 minutes until smooth and elastic (or 8–10 minutes in a stand mixer using a dough hook).

Form the dough into a ball, then place it into a greased deep baking tin (or Pyrex bowl which fits your air fryer) and cover the tin with foil.

Set your air fryer to 40°C (105°F) and put the covered dough inside to prove for 1 hour.

Once the dough has doubled in size, remove it to a lightly floured work surface and roll it out into a rectangle measuring about 30 × 28cm (12 × 11¼in).

Sprinkle the remaining 2 tablespoons of brown sugar over the entire surface of the dough and press it in. Starting at the long side, tightly roll the dough into a long sausage and cut into 6 equal swirls. Place them back into the baking tin, cut-side up, and spaced apart. Cover with foil and return to the air fryer for 45 minutes–1 hour, or until doubled in size.

Remove the rolls and increase the temperature of the air fryer to 150°C (300°F). Brush the bun tops with a little milk, then bake, uncovered, for 25 minutes.

The rolls will have baked into a large round. Carefully tip them out onto a work surface, return them to the air fryer (upside down) and bake again for another 10 minutes.

Makes 6
–
Prep 30 mins,
2 hrs proving
–
Cook 35 mins

ALMOND MERINGUES

These are like delicate little clouds and need to be eaten on the day they are made. I love to decorate them with freeze-dried strawberries and raspberries, but you could also use some dried mango slices from page 12 instead.

2 large egg whites (80g/2¾oz),
    at room temperature
60g (2¼oz) caster (superfine) sugar
60g (2¼oz) icing (confectioners') sugar
½ tsp vanilla bean paste
a few drops of almond extract

To decorate
flaked (slivered) almonds
freeze-dried raspberries or
    strawberries

Whisk the egg whites in a clean, dry bowl until stiff peaks form.

Slowly whisk in the sugars, 1 tablespoon at a time until the mixture is stiff and glossy and no longer feels grainy when rubbed between your fingers.

Whisk in the vanilla bean paste and almond extract.

Preheat the air fryer to 120°C (250°F).

Line 2 oven-style air-fryer racks with baking parchment. Spoon out 8 blobs of meringue, spaced apart, onto the parchment.

Sprinkle with flaked almonds and freeze-dried raspberries or strawberries and bake for 1 hour until crisp on the outside and marshmallow-y in the centre. Swap the racks halfway through cooking to ensure they all cook evenly.

Peel off the paper and serve immediately with some whipped cream, or on their own.

Makes 8
–
Prep 15 mins
–
Cook 1 hr

INDEX

Index

ACKNOWLEDGEMENTS

Firstly to my husband, Chris, my culinary muse and chief taste-tester. Thank you for encouraging me along the way and for being a great team player with all the drop-offs and pick-ups we have to factor in to our working week.

To all my kids, Joni, Wilbur, Gabriel and Clara. You are each wonderful and I am lucky to love you. You always say what you really think of my creations and for that, I am very grateful!

To my lovely friends Rachel, Fern and Edie. Thank for for your friendship and for rescuing me when I needed childcare help. We are going to miss hanging out when you move.

To my dad, stepmum, brothers, sisters-in-law, nieces and nephews, aunties and uncles – it is because of you that I have the confidence to throw myself wholeheartedly into everything I do. To Mum, who lit the touch paper for my love of cooking and good food. I know you are cheering us all on from Heaven!

Stacey, my commissioning editor, who trusted me with this project – thank you so much for your patience and clear vision. You have helped me figure out the content and the shape of this book and have been so accommodating with my family commitments. I think a good editor holds your hand but allows you to run free with your ideas and that is exactly what you have done, so, thank you.

To Vicky – copy editor SUPREME! You were super-speedy with all the edits and extremely gracious when I took my time finishing off the last bits and pieces. Thank you for gently pushing me on – there's nothing like a deadline to kick me into action!

Katie and Rita – what a shoot team! I loved our days together and especially those lunchtime chats. Katie, I love your design, the colours, textures and those CUTE air fryer symbols! Rita, the pro – I really enjoyed working with you, you made sure each shot was the best it could be and I also enjoyed swapping parenting horror stories.

Max – I was very impressed that you found props for some very sparsely written recipes! Thank you for using your creative imagination when I was still in the midst of writing them. All of the props you chose were beautiful.

My able and talented assistants: Ayala, Sophie, Luke and Jemima. You enabled me to focus on making the food look its best while you did all the hard work: washing up, tidying up, clearing the set, loading and unloading the dishwasher, preparing ingredients. This work is unglamorous but essential and I couldn't have done it without you. To my friend and fellow food stylist Evie for helping me find assistants at the last minute and always being at the end of the phone with a helpful tip to a styling question.

Thank you to Salter for providing an oven-style air fryer for me to test on, free of charge.

And, finally, to my younger self who never would have thought I could write one book, let alone two. See, you never know what you can achieve with an opportunity and wonderful people around you.